STEREOPHONICS

YOU GOTTA GO THERE TO COME BACK

STEREOPHONICS
YOU GOTTA GO THERE TO COME BACK

UNIVERSAL MUSIC
PUBLISHING GROUP

Published by:
Universal Music Publishing Group

Exclusive distributors:
Music Sales Limited
Distribution Centre, Newmarket Road,
Bury St. Edmunds Suffolk IP33 3YB, England.
Music Sales Pty Limited
120 Rothschild Avenue, Rosebery, NSW 2018, Australia.

Order No. AM976426
ISBN 0-7119-9817-5
This book © Copyright 2003 by Wise Publications.

Music arrangements by Lucy Holliday, Jack Long & Derek Jones.
Music processed by Paul Ewers Music Design.

Printed in the United Kingdom

www.musicsales.com

Help Me (She's Out Of Her Mind)

Words & Music by Kelly Jones

1. Danc - ing   in the mir - ror,____   yeah, you could see her from a
2. Laugh - ing   all   night;   yeah, she could tell a fun - ny
3. Danc - ing   a - round a low - lit light;____   run - ning rags__ ov - er her

mile, man;   she was al - right.____ She looked right ov - er her
sto - ry,   she could stay up all night.____ Yeah, she was some - one to re-
shoul - ders   red chil - li lights._____ She'd drink you un - der - neath the

shoul - der,   right at me,____ and I was fall - ing through the
mem - ber;   she was black and white.____ Oh, we did it on a
tab - le,   she hold you heavenly tight.____ Slap you right a - cross your

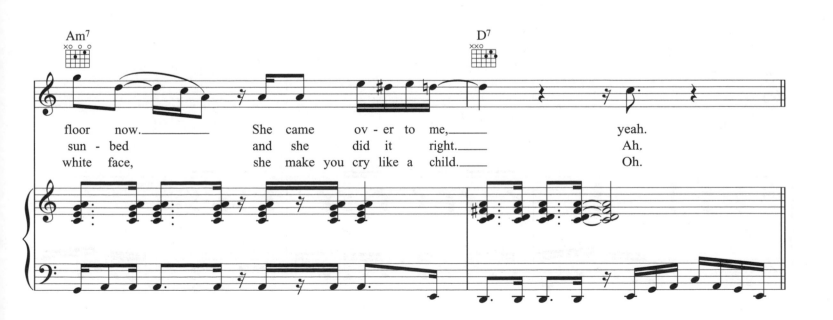

floor now._____ She came ov - er to me,____ yeah.
sun - bed   and she did it right.____ Ah.
white face,   she make you cry like a child.____ Oh.

9

Help me,__ oh help me; she's out of her mind._____
Help me,__ oh help me; she's out of her mind._____
Help me,__ oh help me; she's out of her mind._____

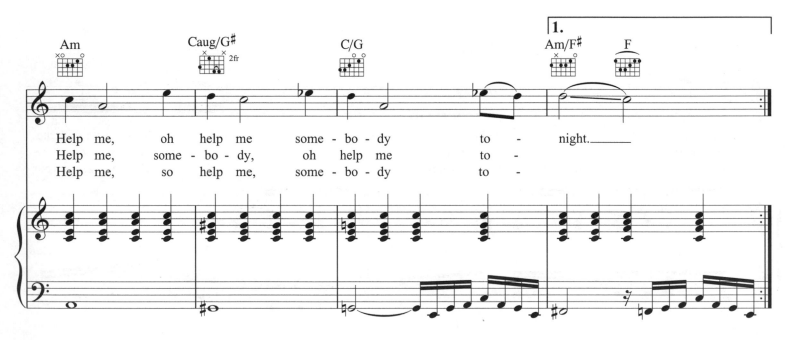

1.

Help me, oh help me some - bo - dy to - night._____
Help me, some - bo - dy, oh help me to -
Help me, so help me, some - bo - dy to -

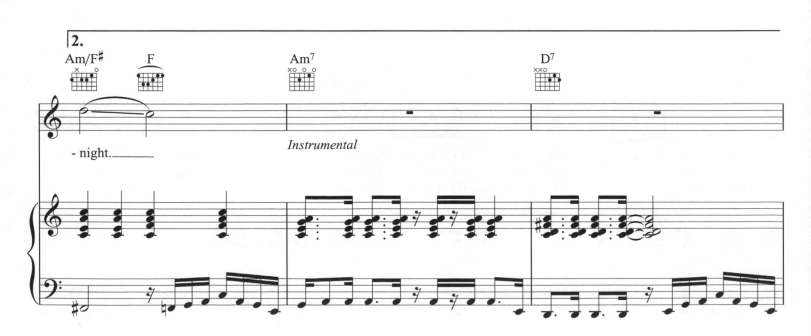

2.

- night._____

Instrumental

Instrumental

4. Cra - zy, out of her mind;_ you wan - na shoot her, wan - na
(5.) fight - ing all the time:_ there's no - thing work - ing, no - thing
(6.) lov - ing on a Sa - tur - day night;_ and mak - ing love un - der a

11

love her,   you can't make up your mind.___   You wan-na tell her all your
gain-ing,   it's just a waste of time.___   You're try-ing hard to re-
blan-ket,   with the tel-ly on loud.___   You wan-na show her that you

sto-ries,   you wan-na op-en your mind.___   You wan-na show her how your
mem-ber   all the beau-ti-ful times,___   but you're cloud-ed by the
love her,   but there's sex on your mind.___   You're mak-ing love from watch-ing

1.

heart works,___   but she ain't got the time.___   5. You're
bull - shit   all of the time.
mov-ies.   I think I'm do-ing it

12

6. Then just right.

Help me, oh help me; she's out of her mind. Help me, so help me, some-body to night.

Repeat ad lib. to fade

13

Maybe Tomorrow

Words & Music by Kelly Jones

1. I've been down and I'm won-de-ring why these lit-tle black clouds keep-a walk-ing a-round with
2. I look a-round at a beau-ti-ful life I've been the up-per side of down, been the in-side of out but we

So may - be to - mor - row I'll find my

way_____ home._____

So may - be_____ to - mor - row, I'll find my

way_____ home.____

Vocal ad lib.

Na, na, na, na. Na, na, na, na. Na, na, na,

na. Na, na, na, na.___ Na, na, na, na_____ oh.____

___ Oh,_____ oh, ah oh.

19

Madame Helga

Words & Music by Kelly Jones

1.Ma- ry, Ma- ry, where___ you been?___
(2.)___ not once,_ not twice___ but three.___

You've been out all night, you ain't got no sleep.
And that's the livin', lovin' wom-an I want me to be.

I've been danc-ing in the hills at a place I know.
There were pic-tures and paint-ings of freaks like me.

She said "And that's the place where the fire-flies glow."
So I drank with my dev-il for my com-pan-y

I saw an In-di-an roll - er_____ to-day on the line._

It was the for-ty-eighth hour_____ we fought our for - ty-eighth fight

At Ma - dame Hel - ga's foll - y_____

1.

To Coda ⊕

is where I spent last night._

2.

2. She been ____

23

24

Jealousy

Words & Music by Kelly Jones

Four___ and twen - ty black_____ boys sing - ing in the street._

2° (white)_____

3° (poor)_____

get - ting high_ on most___ things,_____ wish - ing they were free._

To Coda 1 ✛
To Coda 2 ✛

N.C.

27

I been your preach - er,   I've been your
drunk,_____   I've been your

You Stole My Money Honey

Words & Music by Kelly Jones

1. You stole my mon - ey hon - ey.___ You're cold your blood's___
2. See I'm a giv - er, ta - ker!___ You liked your co -

35

Getaway

Words & Music by Kelly Jones

Do do do do do do do do. Do do do do do do do do.

Do do do do do do do. Do do do do do do do. 1. Re-

-mem - ber when we were ang - els?_____ Be - fore we stole cars and when sex__
(2.) Coppers, rob - bers, cow - boys and Ind - ians,_____ hang - ing round the cor - ner of the

___ and drugs_ lived up___ in a - no - ther world;_____ not a care__
street where you lived; how come it felt so far a - way,_____ just a stone__

be my get-a-way._____ Got-ta get a-way._____

Fly,_____ high_____ be my get-a-way._____

Got-ta get a-way._____

Fly,_____ high_____ be my get-a-way._____

1.
Got-ta get a-way._____

2. C

Climbing The Wall

Words & Music by Kelly Jones

1. I'm just ly - ing here think - ing to my - self a - gain,___
2. I'm just stand - ing here look - ing at my - self a - gain,___
3. Instrumental

I'm round the bend.
I'm go-ing blind.

I've been driv-ing round talk-ing to my-self a-gain,
I'm just sit-ting here play-ing with my-self a-gain,

I'm mak-ing no sense.
it's turn-ing me on.

So what makes you
So what makes yo
So what makes you

I'm Alright
(You Gotta Go There To Come Back)

Words & Music by Kelly Jones

1. I'll drink a-noth-er drink for you,___
2. I'll tell a-noth-er lie for you,___

one, two, three, four, five,___ once I drank a fish a-live.
tell you what you wan-na hear, but that don't make it true.___

I'll drop a-noth-er pill for you,___ six, se-ven, eight, nine, ten,
I'll wear a-noth-er smile for you,___ that way you know I'm fine and

did it be - fore___ I'll do it a - gain.___ I'll tell a - noth - er joke for you,___
hav - ing fun___ with you._____ I'll draw a - noth - er line for you,___
3. I'll take a - noth - er punch for you,___

___ did you hear the one a - bout___ the
___ that way you'll know I'm hip,___ that
___ tie my hands be - hind my back,___ that

one that looks like you? I'll sleep with sleep a - rounds___ for
wat you'll know I'm cool.___ I'll smoke a - noth - er smoke___ for
way you can - not lose. I'll make a - noth - er pound___ for

51

Nothing Precious At All

Words & Music by Kelly Jones

There's a new girl at___ the cof- fee house;___ she got first day
She goes out al- most nine on ev- 'ry night___ and gets high as the

blues.___ She's got red hair and___ a mot-
moon.___ She takes pho- to- graphs of A -

- or - bike___ and lime green shoes,___
-me - ri- can cars where she went to school.___

a mo- hair hat___ and a sum- mer's dress___ and black tat-
She likes fi - re- works___ and can - dle- light___ and fake bad

no-thing pre - cious at all._____

1. **2.**

No-thing pre-cious at all._____ Is she a lon-er___ or a moth-er's girl,_ that's up to

56

you. She got fine lines____ round her ti - red eyes____ and they're paint - ed

blue. She could sleep a - round with an - y - one____ if she want - ed to. Got - ta go, my time is up____

____ right now, got stuff to do.____ *Instrumental*

Rainbows And Pots Of Gold

Words & Music by Kelly Jones

heard you're do-ing well_____ sell-ing art and ev-'ry-thing_

Bm

I knew your num - ber off by heart, it's the

F#m7

on - ly one I like to talk._____ It was - n't me__ us - ing you.__

A add9

Gmaj7

I trust - ed you; one of the few. And we

Bm

had some laughs had some rows_____ but in the end the walls__ came
2° grown a lot since we last spoke, got my - self to - geth - er fixed what was
3° - pose it's dif - fer - ent now it's new,_____ who - ev - er points the fing - er at

F#m7

62

down,   you'd like the place I'm liv - ing now,_____   it's a
broke,   I won - der if we'll talk a - gain?_____   Or_____
who,_____ I real - ly hope you're hap - py both of you_____   And_____

1, 2.   **3.**

shame you can't come a - round._____   And I've   too.
drink to - geth - er just like then._____   I sup -
may - be some - times you'll miss me

Ah,_____   ah,_____   Ah,_____

ah._____

1.   **2.**   *D.S. to fade*

63

High As The Ceiling

Words & Music by Kelly Jones

1. Come on get up high as the ceil - ing, get up on the floor.
2. Come on take my hand if you need me, just knock up - on my door.
3. Come on get up high as the ceil - ing, leave me a light at home.

Think I lost my mind, and my feel - ing I've
You got to stop your mind from dream - ing and
I'm run - ning out of time, and I need it I

68

I Miss You Now

Words & Music by Kelly Jones

right.

die.

I'm

Sad news from to-day's call, and all the pic-tures all in my mind.

help-less, it's gon-na get us; be-fore it gets us I wan-na kiss you good - bye.

I,

I miss you now.

I,

I miss you

71

tell you that you'll be_____ al - right.

I'm help - less, it's gon - na get us;_____ be - fore it

gets us I wan - na kiss you_____ good - bye.

I,_____   I miss you

now._____

I,_____ I miss you now._____

1-3.

4.

rit.

74

Since I Told You It's Over

Words & Music by Kelly Jones

take it back___ you know I___ would.___ I wan - na burn up and die___ so take a look at me)
a - round for long, you got - ta savour what's gone and move your life right a - long,___ so take a look at me)

now,_____ since I told you it's ov - er, you got a hole in your heart.___ I found a four - leaf

clo - ver, you can't tell me this now,_____ this far down the

line_____ that you're nev - er____ ev - er gon - na get ov - er me.

I'm lost, I'm cold__ and get - ting old__ my head__ is full__ of lies__ I

told._____

I've been down, been a - round but I've fal -len on my own two feet and I've left you out__ to drown,__

_____ I nev - er meant for that._____

78

now,_____ since I told you it's ov - er, you got a hole in your

heart._____ I found a four - leaf clo - ver, you can't tell me this

now,_____ this far down the line_____ that you're

Repeat ad lib. to fade

nev - er_____ ev - er gon - na get ov - er me.

79